Poems for the Young at Heart
Love, Infatuation, Patriotism, Inspiration, and Friendship

by

Ltc. Ret. Samuel Lombardo

DORRANCE PUBLISHING CO., INC.
PITTSBURGH, PENNSYLVANIA 15222

The contents of this work including, but not limited to, the accuracy of events, people, and places depicted; opinions expressed; permission to use previously published materials included; and any advice given or actions advocated are solely the responsibility of the author, who assumes all liability for said work and indemnifies the publisher against any claims stemming from publication of the work.

All Rights Reserved
Copyright © 2014 by Ltc. Ret. Samuel Lombardo

No part of this book may be reproduced or transmitted, downloaded, distributed, reverse engineered, or stored in or introduced into any information storage and retrieval system, in any form or by any means, including photocopying and recording, whether electronic or mechanical, now known or hereinafter invented without permission in writing from the publisher.

Dorrance Publishing Co., Inc.
701 Smithfield Street
Pittsburgh, PA 15222
Visit our website at *www.dorrancebookstore.com*

ISBN: 978-1-4349-2989-1
eISBN: 978-1-4349-2340-0

Conversation with Love

Love, you are so beautiful
As no one can describe
When young at heart meet
And their hearts collide
But as time passes by
You're still not shy
You pounce on my heart
And make it run on high
Being alone can be cruel
And you know why
So still, let me love
But also be a friend
With heart and soul complete
To the very end

As the Snowflakes Are Falling

As the snowflakes are falling
And you're not here,
Makes our separation more unbearable
'Cause the passing of another year.
I can't wait until spring
When the skies are blue
And the trees are in bloom
All waiting for you.
I miss your beautiful eyes
And your raven-like hair.
My heart is very painful
And it's more than I can bear.
I know that as soon as winter ends,
It will only be a while,
Until I see your beautiful face
When you return to Carlisle.

I'm in Love with You

As I am still waiting in Destin
Seeing the minutes go by;
To me, they seem like long hours
And can't help time fly by.
So I'll just wait and suffer
Until I see your beautiful smile,
But then, my pain will start all over
'Cause I won't be seeing you for a while.
I'll dispose of my odds and ends
And bid farewell to Carlisle;
Get in my car and speed South
To again see your beautiful smile.
When I think of all the years I've searched
To find someone who I could love,
I know that God works wonders
And arranged our meeting from above.
I look forward to every minute
That I can spend with you,
'Cause my heart keeps telling me
That I am in love with you.

A More Beautiful Woman

As I was sitting down at McGuire's
One Thursday night,
I glanced toward the band
And was struck by the sight,
A more beautiful woman I've never seen.
No matter where I've traveled
Or all the places I've been,
Her soft-mellow eyes
And long waving hair
Shut off everything,
As if no one else was there.
Her slender body awakened
When the local band played;
Like a willow in the wind
Her beautiful body swayed.
I know that I will dream of her
And imagine her swing,
Wishing that she will be back
Before the swallows, in the spring.

A Lonely Ride

*As I was driving down to Knoxville
And on through Tennessee,
I got lonelier and lonelier
'Cause, you were not next to me.
As I continued driving South
With an aching heart,
The pain continued
'Cause we were getting further apart.
Then, I began thinking
About your beautiful smile
And my heart stopped aching
'Cause I was returning to Carlisle.
I can't wait to see you again
With your penetrating eyes
And the stride in your walk
Shifting side to side.
The feeling is so beautiful
And am sure it will not end,
'Cause my heart is full of love
And I will always be your friend.*

My Heart Is in Pain

As I continue waiting
Until I see you again,
Time can't move fast enough
And my heart is in pain.
I'm counting the days
Until you are close to me,
But no matter how time flies
It seems like eternity.
Can't wait until I touch your hands
And see your beautiful smile.
No matter how much I wish
I know it will be a while.
I do hope that time moves faster than it's been,
'Cause my heart keeps hurting
As it continues to spin.
I know when you arrive
My life will begin anew.
And all, it's because
I am in love with you.

My Love for You

As the evening shadows fall
And you are not on my side,
I don't have to tell you
I'm having a lonely ride.
I'll face life, and know it's to be,
That you go on with your life,
But without me.
That does not diminish my love for thee,
    Even though you have a life
    Complete without me.
    So I'll go on living,
    Accepting what life has brought
    With a heart full of loving,
    Though we're living apart.
    I know you understand
    Like the palm of your hand,
That my heart wants to love
But know it just can't.
The pain keeps coming
And it's more than I can bear,
But I'm strong and keep living,
Knowing that you care.
My love, I know will stay to the end,
Knowing in my heart
That you're my very best friend.

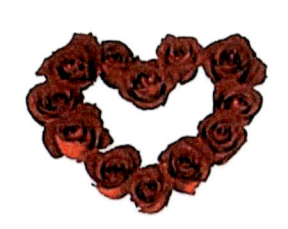

Love at First Sight

I was sipping at the G-Man one night,
Passing the time away,
And when I turned around to look
I was so swept away.
There sat the most beautiful woman
That never came my way.
No matter what I thought,
I didn't know where to begin.
I finally got up my courage,
And approached her with my book,
And in doing so
I took a closer look.
So beautiful and bright
Right then I really knew,
I didn't want her out of sight.
Life, being what it is
I see no different end,
But I feel so fortunate
To have found a new
And beautiful friend.

Lonely, as We Part

*As I'm driving down South
And we're further apart,
My heart gets lonelier
You knew this from the start.*

*So stand by my side
And let me do my thing
'Cause you know like the swallows
I will return in the Spring.
I think of you every minute
Throughout the day
As I'm driving down South
Through Cornelius on the way.
I think of your lips
With passion delight,
And your golden hair
As it reflects the light.
But most of all, are your beautiful eyes
Like two bright starts
Shining in the skies.
My heart is aching
But hoping only for a while
Until I'll see you again
When I return to Carlisle.*

Precious Moments

I pondered all week
Wondering whether I should
And if I invited you
Whether you would.
I finally got up courage
And sent you an e-mail,
Then waited a while
Worrying that I had failed.
Finally, the window lit up
And received your reply.
Immediately, I felt an euphoria
Thinking that I could fly.
I can't thank you enough
For having lunch with me,
And can't help dreaming
That this was meant to be.
Moments like this, are precious and few
Only because I have a few moments
To spend with you.
I thank God every minute
That I have you as a friend,
And you can rest assured
I'll be here till the end.

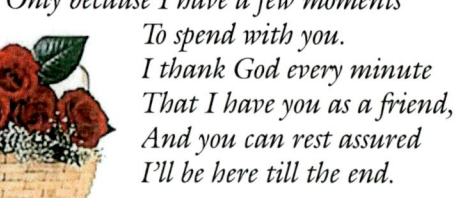

You're the Brightest Star of All

*The sky is full of stars
But only the brightest shine through.
You'll never know how happy I am
That the brightest star is you.
The sky is sometimes stormy
And the storm clouds hide the blue.
But if you're behind some cloud,
You're always ready to break through.
I am not worried about any storm,
Knowing that you're always there,
Otherwise, life would be painful
Much more than I could bear.
I know I can wake up every morning
And wait patiently for night to fall,
'Cause I know when all the stars come out
You'll be the brightest star of all.*

Separation But in Love

It took me awhile to leave Carlisle
'Cause I had to leave my heart behind.
My heart was aching, aching and aching
Way past the Mason-Dixon Line.
Now I must face it
And continue on my way,
'Cause in my heart I know
I'll return one day.
Love, oh love, why did you hit my heart
When you well knew
That we would be apart?
So please stay with me
But don't give me pain,
Because I'll return
Through snow, sleet and rain.
So if you have time
And still want to play,
Let me still love
And I'll make your day!

The Perfect You

*When I think of perfection
I think of only you.
Not only for your beauty
But because of the character in you.
Your beautiful eyes
And raven-like hair
Shut off all else
As if no one else is there.
You're not like others
But dependable to the end,
And I know your determination
Under stress, will not bend.
What this world needs
Are more people like you
Whose words are like gold
And their hearts are true.
I thank God every minute
That I have you as my friend
And you can rest assured
I'm here for you to the end.*

To My Friend Sophia

I went to Alibies last night
To get a bite to eat.
In the hope that I would see you
When you came in to take a seat
I waited and waited
White listening to the karaoke sound,
But my heart continued aching
'Cause you were nowhere around
Finally the door opened
And you walked across the floor.
The entire room lit up
Like I've never seen before
Your soft beautiful eyes
And raven-like hair
Shut off all else
As they filled the air.
I have never been happier
Than when you sat next to me,
As if a hand from heaven
That guided you to me.
My heart stopped aching
When you held my hand,
And our eyes met
I knew you would understand.
Life being what it is
I see no other end
But I thank God every minute
For having you as my friend.

To My Friend Beth

When I walked through the door
And you were not there,
My heart began fluttering
As I went into despair.
Soon the door opened
And you stepped inside,
Walking across the room
With your beautiful stride.
Your soft sparkling eyes
And your hair to the side,
You shut off all else
As if no one else was inside.
Then you told me you're going to Spain;
Again, I felt lonely
And my heart began to pain.
Then learned it would only be awhile
When I can see your beautiful face
On your return to Carlisle.
I thank God every day
For having you as a friend.
You can be assured
I'll be here for you until the end.

To My Beautiful Friend Leslie

I was standing at the bar
Just passing the time away
When I turned around to look
And was almost swept away.
Your stature and physical beauty,
A sight I have never seen
Through all my travels around the world
And all the places I've been.
Your beautiful blue eyes
And waving golden hair
Shut off all else
As if no one was there.
Besides your physical beauty
I sensed that you care,
That you have a soft heart
Just like your golden hair.
I thank God every minute
That I have you as my friend
And you can be assured
That I'm here for you
Until the end.

To My Friend Molly

*I just want to thank you, Molly
For all that you have done.
I don't believe it's any surprise
To me or anyone
The many times we met
You introduced me to everyone.
It was a task to remember all the names
But learned them all, one by one.
All your friends stand very tall
But, of all the people I've ever met
You stand the tallest of all.
I wish you all the best
At whatever you wish to do,
'Cause I know you are a leader
And everyone will follow you.
You will meet many challenges
And I know you'll conquer all,
'Cause I think you'll think of people first
As most important of all.
I feel so very fortunate
To have you as a friend,
And you can rest assured
I'll be here until the end.*

Your God-Given Beauty

When I walked into your salon one day
To keep my appointment for the week
I looked across the room
And was swept off my feet.
Your captivating eyes
And raven-like hair
Shut off everything
As if no one else was there.
Besides your physical beauty,
Your kindness also comes through;
That's why your God-given beauty
Is so complete and true.
You had to have received a calling
To be doing what you do,
And that's to pass onto others
The beauty that's in you.
Life being what it is,
I see no other end,
But to thank God every moment
For having you as a friend.

Your Captivating Eyes

As I walked into Faye's one morning
To get a bite to eat
I then looked up for a minute
And was swept off my feet.
Your captivating eyes
And chestnut brown hair
Shut out everything else
As they filled the air.
I have seen many women before
But none had eyes like you.
They captivate the scenery
And hit me through and through.
Life being what it is,
I see no other end,
But I thank God every minute
To have you as my friend.

A New Friend at Marcello's

As I was sitting down at Marcello's
One Saturday night,
I looked down the aisle
And saw a most beautiful sight.
Her beautiful hair and soft eyes
Radiated across the room
Like Sicilian smiles.
As she walked up to me
And came to a stop,
My heart began fluttering
And spinning like a top.
Then asked for my order
And I didn't know what to say,
'Cause my heart was still spinning
And my mind was in disarray.
So I took my time
And finally made a choice
'Cause what I ate didn't matter
As long, as I heard her voice.
I know now, that I found a beautiful friend
And she can rest assured
That I'll be true
To the end.

Waited to See You

Last night I went to Applebees
Hoping to see you there.
To see your sparkling eyes
And your glowing hair.
I saw many other women
To whom I had talked before,
But none of them made a dent
'Cause, you're the one I adore.
So, I sat there at the booth
Where I saw you, a week ago
And tried to recollect
The night, I saw you glow.
I waited and waited
But you never showed up.
When ten o'clock rolled
around
I decided to give up.
Now, I'm looking forward
To the next time I go,
Hoping to see your beautiful face
With that never-ending glow.
I'm really, really happy
To have returned to Carlisle
And to again see you and
Your beautiful smile.

Two Most Beautiful Friends

I was sitting at the Alibies one night
Just passing the time away.
I then turned around to look
And was almost swept away.
There stood two most beautiful women,
A sight I had never seen,
Through all my travels around the world
And all the places I've been.
I finally got up my courage
And approached them with my book.
In doing so
I took a closer look.
Right then I knew
I didn't want them out of sight,
'Cause they made my evening
So exciting and bright.
Life being what it is
I see no other end,
But I feel I must thank God
For finding me two beautiful friends

Searching for My Love

I have searched the world over
To find a love I can keep.
After searching and searching
The mountain seems so steep.
No matter how difficult the climb
I will never stop.
I'll keep on climbing
Until I reach the top.
Then I will have no more lonely rides
'Cause on every trip,
I'll have my love at my side.
Whether it's peaches and cream
Or sickness or strife
I know that I will love her
The rest of my life.

One Night at the Alibies

*It was still early at the Alibies
And a crowded night,
But you stood above all
Like a beautiful light.
Your deep-set eyes
And raven-like hair
Crowded all else out
And filled the air.
Your slender body
Weaved through the crowd with ease,
Reminding one of a summer breeze.
I wanted to get near you
And get a closer look.
The only course I had
Was to give you my book.
When you gave me a hug
And touched my hand,
I knew right then
That you would understand.
I was struck by your beauty
And your beautiful smile,
And so happy you decided
To study in Carlisle,
Life being what it is
I see no other end
But feel so fortunate
To have you as my friend.*

My New Friend at the G-Man

*I was sitting at the bar
One Saturday night,
When I looked down the aisle
I saw a most beautiful sight.
Her beautiful hair and dark deep eyes,
Radiated across the room, like Sicilian skies.
Then, she walked to me
And came to a stop.
My heart began fluttering
And spun like a top.
She then placed her head
On my shoulder for a while,
She then shed some tears
And drowned them out with a smile.
I am a believer of fate,
As this moment proved to be,
For her, to seek comfort
From a stranger like me.
I feel that God led me
To my new friend,
And know in my heart
We'll be friends to the end.*

Dreaming About You

I live with dreams
Of days gone by
When you were studying in Carlisle
And I caught your eye.
Your dark deep-set eyes
And raven-like hair
Shut off all others
As if no one else was there.
I thank God every minute
For having you as my friend
And you can rest assured
I'll be true until the end.

My Long-Lost Friend

*I searched the world over
For more than a year
My heart was aching
And I hoped you could hear.
As time went on and waiting awhile,
I prayed and prayed
That you would come to Carlisle.
Then, one day the phone rang
And, you were there.
I immediately thanked God
For answering my prayer.
As soon as I saw you,
My heart stood still,
As if I had just climbed
A very steep hill.
I am so happy that you called
Even though after a long while,
So that again I can see
Your beautiful smile.
I thank God every day
That I have found you again,
And to have you as
One of my best friends.*

Meeting You at McGuire's

*I went to McGuire's one evening
To get a bite to eat.
When I turned around to look
I was swept off my feet.
When I saw your beautiful eyes
And your waving hair
You shut off everyone else
As if no one was there.
Finally we started talking
And you touched my hand;
When I looked into your eyes
I knew you would understand.
We talked for an hour
And had not yet ordered a drink,
'Cause I was up in cloud nine
And forgot how to think.
I'm so happy that I stopped at McGuire's
And found a woman that's true.
I thank God every minute
That finally I found you.*

My New Friend Lisa

*I invited my new friend Lisa
To a party with you and friends,
Wondering if something would happen
To close some open ends.
The party went on and on
But there was never a spark.
I felt that my heart knew this
Right from the start.
I was also thinking that
We could engage in a dance,
But love kept butting in
And Lisa didn't have a chance.
I know now <u>for sure</u>
That I cannot change my course,
From the one my heart has started
Whether it's for better or for worse.
So, I accept that I can't go farther
To make my life complete.
Just seeing your smile, once in a while,
Will always be with me to keep.
All I ask you as a friend
Is that you fully understand
That my love for you is true
And I am here for you, to the very end.*

My New Friend at the Barracks

When I climbed the stairs
And opened the door,
I went into shock
And almost fell to the floor.
Sitting at the desk
Was the most beautiful girl.
I felt an euphoria
That I had never felt before.
Her deep, but soft eyes, and beautiful hair
Were so overwhelming
That they crowded the air.
I learned then that she was taken
And to my dismay,
My heart was shaken,
So I continued on my way.
Now, I must accept life
For what I have been dealt
And thank God every minute
For the euphoria I felt.
And know in my heart,
That I have found a new friend.
She can be rest assured
That I'll be true to the end.

My New Friend At the G-Man

*As I walked down the aisle
At the Gingerbread Man,
I squeezed through the crowd
As fast as I could.
And when your eyes met
I knew you understood.
I was sent into ecstasy
Of which I never knew before,
And knew right then
That I wanted to see you more.
While I was near you
I felt so very good
And knew right away
That you also, understood.
I just can't wait until the next time
When, again, I'll see your eyes,
And your hair so fine,
That we can enjoy dinner
And also some wine.
I feel so lucky that I met
Such a beautiful friend
To whom I can be true
To the very end.*

Missing You

I went to your pavilion
To see a thing or two,
But the main reason for going
Was to get a glimpse of you.
I waited and waited
But you were nowhere around;
Also listened for your voice
But never heard that sound.
As the wait became longer
My heart began to ache,
'Cause I really missed seeing
Your beautiful face.
I picked this day
Since you're normally there,
But not seeing your presence
Was more than I could bear.
So I'll try again tomorrow
As my heart continues in pain;
You can be rest assured I'll be there
Through snow, sleet, or rain.

Meeting Beautiful Diane

I went to McGuire's last night
To get a bite to eat.
When I turned around to look
I was almost swept off my feet;
There stood the most beautiful woman
I had ever seen.
No mater where I've traveled
Or all the places I've been,
Here soft blue almond eyes
And waving golden hair
Shut off everything
As if no one else was there.
I wanted so badly to talk to her
But didn't know whether she would,
But then, when our eyes met
I knew that she understood.
I thank God every minute
For having Diane as a friend
And she can be rest assured
That I'll be true to the end.

My Beautiful New Orleans Friend

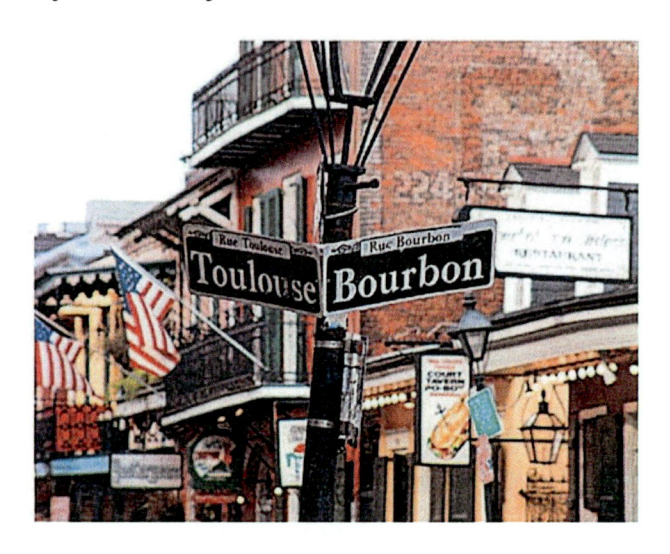

As I walked into AJ's last evening
To get a bite to eat,
I looked up for a moment
And was swept off my feet.
Your striking beauty,
The likes I'd never seen before,
Struck me like a rock
As I walked across the floor.
Your captivating eyes
And raven-like hair
Shut off all else
As if no one was there.
I have seen many beautiful women,
But none had eyes like you.
They captivated the scene
And hit me through and through.
I thank God every minute
That I have you as my friend
And just like the swallows;
I hope that you'll return in the Spring.

Waited and Waited

I waited by the entrance
Most of the day
Hoping to see you
If you came my way.
Time came and went
And you still didn't show.
All I could think of
Were things you should know.
Like how you struck me
With your beauty and grace,
Your soft blue eyes,
And angelic face.
It was more then just physical
With your golden hair;
I sensed a soft heart
Of a person who cares.
With a heavy and broken heart
I must return to Carlisle
And hoping that it won't be long
Until I see your beautiful smile.

It's Been a Long Time Waiting

*It's been a long time waiting
Until your birthday arrived,
And now I really wonder
How I managed to survive,
To celebrate your birthday
I know, it's special for you,
But, no matter how many times you celebrate
I'll always be waiting for you.
Your golden hair and soft blue eyes
Are still beautiful and the same.
They keep my heart throbbing
And now, I know who to blame.
I tried so hard to shrug it off
'Cause there's no way to follow through.
I can only wait for your next birthday
Because I'll always be in love with you.*

Graduation Day

*I could not help but notice
Your beautiful hair
When you walked up the path
And on up the stairs.
You received your degree
And then turned around
To smile at your friends,
Who were showing their approval
With an applauding sound.
Now, you'll be facing life
With a degree in your hand
And face many challenges
Some of which you won't understand.
I know you'll succeed
At whatever you try,
But knowing that you're leaving
My heart wants to cry.
But I'll try to resist it,
Although in pain for a while,
Knowing that one day in the future
You'll be returning to Carlisle.*

Finding a New Friend

After searching the world over
And no one could be found,
I finally found a woman
With her feet on the ground.
Besides being patriotic
And a lover of country and flag,
We think so much alike
That a better friend couldn't be had.
She loves her entire family
And works around the yard,
I don't know of any other woman
That works so very hard.
I hope that she will have some time
To have a dinner or two,
So that we can get better acquainted
And enjoy some good times too.
I feel so very fortunate
To finding such a friend.
She can rest assured, that I
Will be here to the end.

Enjoying Each Other

*I was sitting by my computer
Feeling somewhat blue
An e-mail then appeared
And was so happy, it was from you.
My heart started pumping faster
And I am sure, this is true
That all this is happening
'Cause, I'm in love with you.
When you said, you had some time
To have a lunch or two,
I became so much happier
'Cause my dream came true.
The only hardship I face is,
That lunch is a week away.
But I know it's worthwhile waiting
To hear what you have to say.
We can have lunch in the borough
Then, come home and spend some time.
'Cause, every moment I spend with you
I consider it divine.
I know we'll enjoy each other
As no one can explain,
Even for a short moment
Over a glass of champagne.*

Driving Over to See You

As I drove over the bridge,
Across the Emerald Bay,
My heart started pumping faster
'Cause you weren't too far away.
Arriving I sat down to eat
Waiting to see your face,
'Cause it's been too long since I saw you last,
And it's about all I can take.
But I was so disappointed
When I learned you were off that day
And my heart got more painful
As I counted the minutes away.
I hope that we can meet more often
So that I can see your beautiful face
And maybe have a dinner or two
At your favorite place.
I'm sorry that I have to leave now,
Since my heart is in pain,
Knowing that it will keep aching
Until I see you again.

Driving East on Legion

*As I was driving east on Legion
With the morning sun shining through,
I found myself driving faster
Knowing that soon I'd be seeing you.
Your penetrating eyes
And chestnut brown hair
Takes up all the space
And permeates the air.
I have never enjoyed breakfast
Like the one at our Legion Hall,
'Cause no matter what food is served
It's because of you, most of all.
I can't wait until next Sunday
Knowing that breakfast is in wait,
But then, eating isn't that important
As long as I see your face.
I know that a week is long to wait
Until I see you again,
Knowing that my heart is begging
And it's in continuous pain.
But I'll weather the storm
To the very end,
Knowing that driving east on Legion
I will always have a friend.*

Finding a Friend

I don't know whether I heard it
Or it's just lore,
That you can't fall in love
If you're past eighty-four.
I find the young too young
And the old too old
And the one in-between
Have been taken I'm told.
So, I'll go on living
Enjoying the beauty at hand
And know that most people
Will understand.
I'll treat everyone right
To the very end;
If I don't find love
I know I'll find a friend.

Breakfast at the Legion

*It was early Sunday morning
When I went to the Legion to eat.
As I sat down, I looked up
And was swept off my feet.
Her raven-like hair
And beautiful smile
Pushed back breakfast
For quite a while.
Breakfast was not important
As long as she was there,
'Cause her smile shut off all others
As if no one else was there.
I'm so happy I went to the Legion
To have breakfast on this day,
'Cause such a beautiful woman was there,
That made it a special day.*

Breakfast at Dennys

It was early one Sunday morning
And I was up and around.
I was thinking of eating Breakfast
Somewhere in town.
So I asked my neighbor
Who had been here awhile.
He told me the best was Dennys
Down the road about a mile.
So I took off down the road
Which was still blanketed with fog.
All I saw were neighbors
Walking their dogs.
I finally got to Dennys
And found it full of noise
And soon it was understandable
'Cause it was full of girls and boys.
So I ate my breakfast, which was very good,
And know it was so tasteful
That I ate more than I should.
So I drove back to my area
This time I found no fog
And to my surprise
I didn't see a dog.

A Night Out at Carrabbas

*I went to Carrabbas the other night
To see what their Italian food was like.
Waiters and waitresses were in great demand
'Cause it was full of diners from Disneyland.
As I looked over the menu with great delight
I saw Chicken Marsala, which I really like.
So, I ordered the chicken and a little wine
And settled down to really dine.
Upon eating the chicken and thought I was through
I didn't think it was complete without Tiramisu.
Upon completion, I went on my way,
Satisfied to tell others to also come this way.*

A Beautiful Evening in Destin

One evening I went to The Boathouse,
To get a bite to eat.
When I entered and took a look.
I was almost swept off my feet.
Her stature and physical beauty,
A sight I have never seen,
Through all my travels around the world,
And all the places I have been.
She then invited me to Hogs,
I didn't know what to say,
But looking at her beauty,
I just couldn't stay away.
Her beautiful eyes and golden hair
Shut off all else,
As if no one was there.
We then danced to the music at hand,
And when I held her close,
I knew she would understand.
Besides her being beautiful,
I felt that she cared.
That she had a soft heart,
Just like her golden hair.
The evening was so beautiful,
And thank God for a new friend,
She can rest assured
I'll be a true friend
Through the very end.

A Beautiful Evening at Marcello's

*As I was eating at Marcello's
And having a sip of wine
I looked up for a moment
And saw you standing in line
Your beautiful eyes
And raven-like hair
Obscured all others
As if not one else was there.
I'm so happy that you accepted
To sit down next to me,
Right then I felt an euphoria
As if our meeting was meant to be.
What a beautiful evening at Marcello's
More than words that I can say.
Together with meeting Bradyn
And joining him at play.
I can't wait until the next time
When we're together again.
I thank God every minute
That I have you as my friend.*

Your First Golf Lesson

As you took your position
To swing your first club,
I could not help thinking
That I wanted to give you a hug.
'Cause you took a great step
Towards your future life
Where work can be strenuous
And life in general, full of strife.
Golf will give you comfort
And relief from stress of life.
It can be intimidating
And humiliating too
When the swing is not working
And you think it's only you.
But keep on swinging
Even though it's not your best.
'Cause all the benefits you'll receive
Will overcome the rest.
So, as you keep on swinging
Through all the pain and strife,
Just remember it's the only great sport
That you can play
The rest of your life.

Eating at Dewey Destin

When you are visiting Destin
And looking for a place to eat,
You must visit Dewey Destin
Because you are in for a treat.
From the blackened grouper
To the trigger on the grill,
Whatever you select to eat
You are in for a thrill.

Their personnel are very friendly
And all will meet you with a smile.
The view is also the greatest
That you want to stay a while.
So the next time you visit Destin
And you casually want to eat,
Make sure you visit Dewey Destin
'Cause you're in for a treat.

Not a Night for Red Roses

I went to Alibies one evening
To get a beer and a bite to eat.
When I looked across the crowded room
I was almost swept off my feet.
There stood two most stunning women of a kind
Of which I thought I would never find.
When we looked in each other's eyes
And then able to touch their hand,
If they then felt like I did
I would know they would understand.
We then planned to go to Marcello's
And were to meet, on Sunday night.
So, on Sunday evening, I waited and waited
But they were nowhere in sight.
I had brought them red roses
And looking forward to a beautiful night.
But when neither showed up
I threw them away and out of my sight.
To say the least my heart was broken
When they didn't show.
It was not a night for red roses
And lost a beautiful night, we'll never know.

My First Valentine's Day in Destin

*It's my first Valentine's Day in Destin
and love I haven't found.
Maybe it's because of my age
And there's no one my age around.
The young are too young
And the old too old
And the one's in between
Are absent I'm told.
But I'm still very happy
'Cause of Destin which I've found,
With its beautiful emerald waters
And friendly people around.
I know I'll never be lonely
'Cause, in Destin is where I'll stay
And know that I'll find love
By the next Valentine's Day.*

Alone on Valentine Day

*I went to a restaurant
On this Valentine Day
To have a special dinner
On this beautiful day.
Not to my surprise
There was a crowd at the door,
All waiting for dinner
And possibly more.
So I was called to my table
When it was my time,
And saw mostly couples
Sipping on their wine.
My dinner was great
And the Merlot was divine.
But seeing all the beautiful women
Not one was mine.
So I ate in a hurry
And returned home to stay.
Hoping that next year,
I will not be alone
On Valentine Day.*

Breaking a Promise

*I was looking forward to dinner
That AHEC has once a year.
We waited a month
And now the time was getting near.
Just three days before the date,
You said you couldn't attend,
'Cause your friend from Jamaica
Was coming for an event.
The event was his birthday
On which he was thirty-seven
And a few moments with him
Must made you feel you were in heaven.
After my long life,
It's very easy for me to see,
That what he had to offer
Was better than being with me.
So keep on doing
What you think is good for you,
But remember that promises
Are very important too.
That a few moments of ecstasy
Are only temporary while in flight,
But good friends that you make
Are with you for life.*

Waited All Evening

*I waited all evening
Impatiently for you.
The time came and went
But you never came through.
Thank you for calling
To let me know.
However, the pain still lingers
Since my heart received the blow.
It's difficult to say
When both of us have the time,
To go out some evening
And have dinner with some wine.
Until that day comes,
I do want to say,
That we'll just have to wait
For another day.*

The Night of the Butterfly

*The memorable night our lips met
I wished it would never end.
You then told me, you were a butterfly
And flew away around the bend.
I hope that of all the flowers you see,
You'll find one that fits your style.
So that you don't have to keep flying
Dropping each one off, after only a while
You may think you're happy and free,
But a moment or two of ecstasy
Is not what you think it to be.
It's only love of heart and soul
That can give you lasting peace.
No matter how many flowers you pick
They will only act to tease.
In the meantime, keep flying around
And enjoy the flowers at hand.
Maybe as time goes on
You'll come to understand.
I do wish the best for you, but regret
That it's difficult for you to see,
That the right flower you passed up
Was really me.*

Shopping at Winn-Dixie

Driving East on Mountain
Going shopping for awhile,
I can't wait to reach Wynn-Dixie
To see your beautiful smile.
Your captivating eyes
And chestnut-brown hair
Shut off all else
And I forget why I'm there.
Awakening and walking down the aisles,
I can't wait to complete my shopping
And return to see your beautiful eyes.

Departing, but hoping for tomorrow;
That again you'll be there.
'Cause, if you're absent
The pain is more than I can bear.
Life, being what it is
I foresee no other end;
But, I'm thankful every moment
For having you as my friend.

Going to McGuire's

*When I arrived in Destin
And didn't know where to go,
I stopped at McGuire's
And haven't let go.
With all the good food on hand
And the money on the wall,
They have all the drinks one wants
But, their own beer, is best of all.*

*Their personnel are the greatest
With their service and a smile
One has to have a second beer
And socialize awhile.
So if you are visiting Destin
And going out while you're here,
You just have to stop at McGuire's
'Cause you won't find a better beer.*

Shopping in Florida

I went shopping at the Walmart today
And was very much surprised,
That the long line in front
Was either bald or gray.
So I paid the cashier
And went on my way
To complete my shopping
For the rest of the day.
I tried CVS, which was on the way,
And found the lines longer
Waiting to pay
For their senior medication
That were on display.
So no matter where I went
Throughout the day,
I saw no young people
Either shopping or at play.
So I came to the conclusion
That this was not my place to stay,
Until a few more years
When I'll be either bald or gray.

My Best Christmas Day

I was in Destin, Florida this Christmastime,
Alone, not knowing what to do;
And then my friend Vandi
With an invitation came through.
She invited me to Biloxi
Where the rest of the family stays.
She drove us along with Daniel
So as to be there on Christmas Day.
I met the entire family,
Including the children at play,
Who came to celebrate with family
In the old American Southern way.
As we all sat to dinner,
Which was preceded with a prayer,
I couldn't help admire the table
With Southern food, layer on layer.
As I look back on the Holy day
And all the new friends I have,
I believe it was a hand from Heaven
For all the things it gave.
No matter how many years will pass
And all the holidays along the way,
I will always remember this as being
My best Christmas Day.

Getting Old

I remember when on the kitchen table
Were jams, jellies, and cake.
But now that I'm getting old
All I see are the pills I take.
There's Metamucil and fiber foods
And minerals that I must choose.
But I remember the day
When all I drank was juice.
There is also glucosamine
And all the pills for pain,
Because with each year
My arthritis seems to gain.
So now I know that I must slow down
Even though I feel bold,
I have to come to realize
That I am also getting old.

I Am Not a Computer Man

*I'll use the telephone
And write when I can,
And I know for sure
I'm not a computer man.
I know it's handy
To leave a message or two,
But when you turn it on
A voice does not come through.
The voice is not there
And cannot be felt
Because the words are typed
And come through the internet.
So I'll stick to my telephone
Where I can hear my friends' voice,
And I am so happy
That this medium is my choice.
The computers can go ahead
And do their own thing,
But I know they can't tell
Whether its winter or spring.
I know they have a place
In the business they do,
But they will never impart the feeling
That can be warm and true.
So I'll continue using the phone
As much as I can
And accept the fact
That I am not a computer man.*

Washington's Birthday

*It means so much to our nation
To celebrate our Father's Day,
But Congress had to change it
And now it's called President's Day.
I don't know what they were thinking
When they voted their way.
I believe it was more about business
Than respect for our Patriot's Day.
I don't know if they realize
What it means to our children
To honor our Father's Day,
'Cause if they don't restore it
It will be forgotten with each passing day.
If we want to preserve our nation
And nurture patriotism in some way,
Congress had better restore
George Washington's Birthday.*

The Truth Shall Set You Free

The truth shall set you free
You can be assured that's what you'll hear
When you go out with me.
We sometimes make excuses
For something we do or say
Knowing that we didn't say all
So that things would go our way.
Remember that when we lie a bit
And we think it's okay,
It will only put us in prison
And it will never go away.
So just think it over a bit
Before you wish to flee,
'Cause, no matter how you cover it up
It's only the truth, that shall set you free.

This Is Memorial Day

*This is Memorial Day
In our land of the free.
It's because of those who sacrificed
Whose graves you're here to see.
They fought on foreign lands
And across the open sea,
And paid the ultimate price
To keep you and I free.
So put all things aside
And honor this important day,
Which we have dedicated
As our Memorial Day.*

Say "Thanks" on Veterans Day

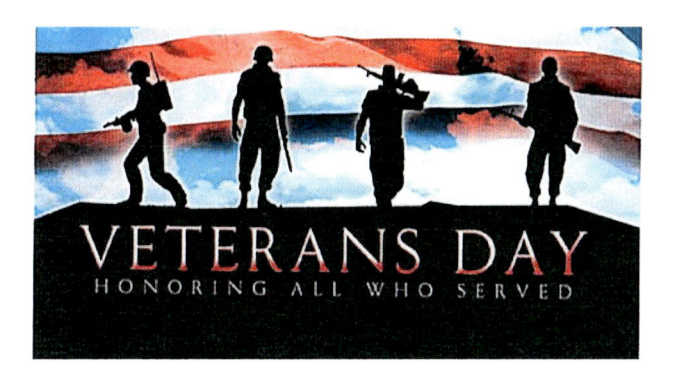

On this Day of Remembrance
Now called Veterans Day,
I went and had lunch
At one of our local cafes.
There, I saw some old friends
Who also came to town today.
And when they all saw me
They said "Happy Veterans Day."
As soon as I was seated
I didn't know what to say,
'Cause I didn't think it was right
To say "Happy" Veterans Day.
On this day of remembrance
When we honor those who fought,
To show our appreciation
"<u>Thanks</u>" Was a better word, I thought.
But we should honor all veterans
No matter how they served.
Because they all contributed
And our thanks they now deserve.
So, from now on, when you meet a veteran
No matter what time of day,
Shake his or her hand
And say "Thanks" on Veterans Day.

Give Me Back My America

Give me back my America
The one I used to know.
The one I fought so hard for
Through rain, ice and snow.
Give me back my America
Where everyone was free
From taxes on everything
From milk, coffee, and tea.
Give me back my America
Where the majority was on top
And the minority worked extra hard
To reach the goal they sought.
I feel that we are slipping into socialism

Where everyone's the same.
And most of us will lose our freedoms
And our leaders have no shame.
Let us go back to our original roots
That our forefathers sought,
And achieved our freedoms
'Cause of all the wars we fought.
Wake up America
Before it's too late.
Vote out all the liberals
'Cause there is so much at stake.
If you carry out your duty
And vote the right way,
We'll bring back our America
And our freedoms will be here to stay.

My Friend Danielle

*When I looked at my E-mail
And saw that it was from you,
I almost fell over
Wondering whether it was true.
I remember your beauty
Since it was so rare;
With your soft blue eyes
And waving golden hair.
I am so happy that you are
Doing what you like best,
And I know that in time
You will learn all the rest.
I keep punching myself
To realize that this is true;
That after all this time
I again heard from you.
I want to thank you so much
For taking the time
By sending me an E-mail
And getting online.
I thank God every minute
For having you as my friend;
You can also rest assured
I'll be a true friend to the end.*